cloverleaf books™

Our American Symbols

Is a Bald Eagle Really Bald?

Martha E. H. Rustad

illustrated by Holli Conger

M MILLBROOK PRESS · MINNEAPOLIS

For Marlow and Vonnie —M.E.H.R.

For my Uncle Kenneth, whose time
has been well spent with the eagles
—H.C.

Millbrook Press
A division of Lerner Publishing Group, Inc.
241 First Avenue North
Minneapolis, MN 55401 USA

For updated reading levels and more information, look up this
title at www.lernerbooks.com.

The images in this book are used with the permission of:
© Chris Hill/Shutterstock.com

Main body text set in Slappy Inline 18/28.
Typeface provided by T26.

Library of Congress Cataloging-in-Publication Data

Rustad, Martha E. H. (Martha Elizabeth Hillman), 1975–
    Is a bald eagle really bald? / by Martha E. H. Rustad ;
illustrated by Holli Conger.
        pages   cm. — (Cloverleaf books. Our American
symbols)
    Includes index.
    ISBN: 978-1-4677-2138-7 (lib. bdg. : alk. paper)
    ISBN: 978-1-4677-4771-4 (eBook)
    1. Bald eagle—Juvenile literature. I. Conger, Holli, illustrator.
II. Title.
QL696.F32R87 2015
598.9'43—dc23   2013042059

Manufactured in the United States of America
1 – BP – 7/15/14

TABLE OF CONTENTS

Chapter One
An American Mascot

Our class is having a visitor today!
Ms. Patel makes us guess who.

"Our visitor eats fish," she hints.

"Is it my dad?" asks Anabelle.

"No," says our teacher. "It has a
sharp beak and feathers."

Joshua guesses, "Is it a duck?"

"No, but it is a bird. What bird do you see on this dollar?" asks Ms. Patel.

"A bald eagle!" says Rose.

"That's right!" answers Ms. Patel.

"Why is a bald eagle on that dollar?" asks Natalie.
"The bald eagle is a **symbol** of our **country**,"
says Ms. Patel.

"What's a symbol?" asks John.

"A symbol is something that stands for something
else," answers our teacher. "Like a bear is a
symbol of our school. We call the bear our mascot,
which is like a symbol."

· Bald Eagle ·

· Bald Eagle ·

Bald eagles are important to many American Indian cultures. They believe bald eagles carry messages to gods. Bald eagle feathers are treasured gifts.

We learn that eagles have been symbols in other places too. They appeared on coins long ago in Greece and Rome.

"The bald eagle is also on **the Great Seal**," Ms. Patel tells us.

"A seal is visiting too?" Luke asks.

"No, Luke," our teacher laughs. "The Great Seal is a picture. It is a way to show that something is **officially American**."

The Great Seal has been a symbol of the United States since 1782.

We learn the Great Seal has been on money and stamps. It's also on government buildings and important papers. Some soldiers have the Great Seal on the buttons of their uniforms.

"Look closely at the Great Seal," says Ms. Patel. "What is the bald eagle holding in its feet?"

"I see a plant!" says Karen.

"Right," says Ms. Patel. "It's an **olive branch**. It stands for **peace**."

"I see arrows!" says Noah.

"The **arrows** are for **strength**," explains Ms. Patel.

A banner in the bald eagle's mouth reads *E pluribus unum*. These Latin words mean, "one from many." It's a way of saying that many states make one country.

THE GREAT SEAL

"Why are there stars on top?" asks Kevin.

"There are **thirteen stars**," says Ms. Patel. "That's because our country started out with **thirteen states**."

·US EMI

Chapter Two

A Feathered Visitor

Knock, knock! A woman walks in with a big box. "That looks like my dog's kennel!" whispers Sophia.

"Hello, class!" says the woman. "I'm Dr. Kelly. I brought a bald eagle to meet you today. His name is Sam. He's from the **raptor center**."

We all have to sit still so we don't scare Sam.
Dr. Kelly puts on a glove to protect her hand
from the **talons** on his feet.

Raptors are birds that kill and eat other animals for food. Raptor centers take care of wild birds that are hurt or sick. Some birds return to the wild. Others stay at the raptor center.

Adult bald eagles weigh about 10 pounds (4.5 kilograms). Their wings stretch out as wide as 8 feet (2.4 meters).

Dr. Kelly takes Sam out of the box.

"He's huge!" says Kyra.

Jackson pipes up, "Didn't you say he was bald?"

"Good question," says Dr. Kelly. "The *bald* part of its name comes from the word *piebald*. It means 'having white marks.'"

We admire Sam's white and brown feathers.

Sam's bright yellow eyes watch us.

"Bald eagles have very good **eyesight**," says Dr. Kelly. "They soar high in the sky. Their eyes see food far below. Then they dive down to catch it."

"Where do they take the food?" asks Oliver.

Dr. Kelly says, "They can swallow it whole in the air."

"That's fast food!" says Penny.

"Yes," Dr. Kelly grins. "They also bring it to their babies in their nests."

We learn that eagles are not picky eaters. They eat fish, birds, small mammals, snakes, turtles, and even dead animals.

Chapter Three

A Fitting Symbol

"Why is the bald eagle our country's **mascot**?" asks Harry.

"I know!" says Lily. "Because they fly free. And **Americans are free**."

"Good answer," Ms. Patel says. "Also, bald eagles live only in **North America**."

In the late 1800s and the 1900s, the number of bald eagles shrank. Hunters killed some. Chemicals used on farms made their eggshells weak. So the government passed laws to keep them safe.

Bald Eagle Range Map

Year-round

Summer (Breeding)

Winter (Nonbreeding)

"All right, everyone, we're out of time," our teacher says. "Line up for lunch. Fish is on today's menu."

Connie says, "Hey, that's what bald eagles like to eat!"

"What do we tell Dr. Kelly and Sam?" Ms. Patel asks.

"Thank you, Dr. Kelly! Good-bye, Sam!" we all say together.

My Own Mascot

A mascot is a symbol of a group. Teams often have mascots that help cheer. Pick an animal or a symbol to be your own mascot.

What You Need:

paper
crayons

1) Think about your favorite activity or one of your talents. Are you a swimmer? A reader? A singer? A loyal friend? A runner?

2) Think of an animal or character that has the same talent. For example, dolphins are strong swimmers. People see owls as smart animals. Robins sing. Dogs are loyal. Cheetahs run fast.

3) Draw a picture of the animal doing your favorite activity. Write the first letter of your name on the animal.

GLOSSARY

chemicals: substances that are found in nature or made by science

government: a group of people that make rules for a country

hunter: someone who finds and kills an animal

mascot: an animal or person that is a symbol of a group

raptor: a kind of bird that hunts

symbol: an object that represents something else

talons: sharp claws on a bird's foot

treasured: highly valued

This bald eagle is
about to take flight.

BOOKS

Eldridge, Alison, and Stephen Eldridge. *The Bald Eagle: An American Symbol.*
Berkeley Heights, NJ: Enslow Elementary, 2012.
Photographs and simple text tell more about our national bird.

George, Jean Craighead. *The Eagles Are Back.* New York: Dial, 2013.
This picture book tells how eagles came back from the brink of extinction.

WEBSITES

All about Birds: Bald Eagle
http://www.allaboutbirds.org/guide/bald_eagle/sounds
Listen to sounds made by bald eagles.

Birds of Prey: Bald Eagle Webcam Highlights
http://video.nationalgeographic.com/video/animals/birds-animals/birds-of
-prey/dc-eaglecam-highlights/
Watch video clips of bald eagles and their young in their nest in
Washington, DC.

Symbols of the US Government
http://bensguide.gpo.gov/k-2/symbols/index.html
This website from the US Government Printing Office tells about
famous symbols of the US government.

LERNER SOURCE™
Expand learning beyond the printed book. Download free, complementary educational resources for this book from our website, www.lerneresource.com.